KROWD

REVIEW

WINTER

2015

Editor-in-chief **Noga Sklar**
Literary editor **Rachel Hildebrandt**
Cover design **KBR**
Cover illustration *Shivering Girl with a Blue Ring*, oil on canvas by Jozsef
Rippl-Ronai, 1916

ISBN: 978-1-944608-10-1
ISBN: 978-1-944608-11-8 (E-book)

KBR Digital Publishers LLC.
www.kbrdigital.com
www.facebook.com/kbrdigital
contact@kbrdigital.com

Greenville - SC
1|864|373.4528

LCO000000 Literary Collections

Shivering Girl with a Blue Ring, oil on canvas by Jozsef Rippl-Ronai, 1916.

WINTER

A
NOTE
FROM
THE
EDITOR

Dear reader,

The journal you have now in hand represents a pivotal moment in my career as a writer and editor, the great achievement of a lifetime.

For the last ten years, I have been faced with the challenges of a bicultural marriage, and although I could read and speak English (with a Latino accent) since I was a child, some internal reluctance stopped me from writing in this language. And for all this time my husband could not understand what I wrote, which meant he could not really understand me.

Going back in time to my childhood in Brazil, my grandmother was an immigrant from Palestine who could never read or write Portuguese, therefore living most of her life as a semi-aware foreigner, continuously mocked by us, merciless children, because of her strong accent and funny Yiddish expressions. Which, by the way, I keep alive in my memory, and use here and there to add a special flavor to my writing.

It was only a year ago, after moving to the United States, that something inside made me pursue the dream of making myself understood to a wider audience. English, as you all know, is the dominant, "universal" language today.

I started by hiring a translator to create my works in English, but being a perfectionist and very demanding, I was only happy when I decided to translate them myself; *et voilà*, I have been contaminated by the "translating fever," the desire to dedicate myself to the task of guiding readers across the bridge of understanding, to enjoy other cultures, other dreams. In other words, to travel abroad in the pages of a book.

And here we are.

Before you move forward, I wish to acknowledge the door that was opened to me when I met Rachel Hildebrandt, a literary translator from German. She has not only doubled the scope of possible future publications, enriching the multicultural aspect of KBR-US, but she has also made my writing clearer and allowed me to dive even deeper in search of my roots.

Have a nice journey!

DARLING

WOLFGANG HERMANN
AUSTRIA

Born in 1961 in Bregenz, Austria, **Wolfgang Hermann** studied philosophy in Vienna, after which he traveled extensively and lived in Berlin, Paris, Aix en Provence, and Tokyo. He has published numerous books of prose and poetry, among the most recent: *Abschied ohne Ende* (novel, 2012), *Schatten auf dem Weg durch den Bernsteinwald* (poetry, 2013), *Die Kunst des unterirdischen Fliegens* (novel, 2015), and *Die letzten Gesänge* (stories, 2015). Wolfgang Hermann's numerous prizes include the Juergen Ponto Prize (1987), the Siemens Literature Prize (2002), the Anton Wildgans Prize (2006), and the Austrian State Advancement Award (2007). *Herr Faustini takes a Trip* is the first of his books to be published in English.

Translated by **Rachel Hildebrandt**

for L.

It was a winter evening. That afternoon I had watched the seagulls stalk across the ice in the harbor. I was sitting over a beer in Caruso, although I think it's called Viva today. I was all by myself there, which back then didn't happen all that often because I had friends, or at least I thought I did. Whatever the case, there was always a crowd of people around me. I was a bit more youthful and attractive than I am today, perhaps that was the reason. Or maybe it's just that the times have changed, although there still seem to be plenty of folks to just sit around and kill time with. Anyway, I was sitting in Caruso when the door opened, and there she stood. It's not like I believe in predestination or anything like that, but as she just stood there and looked around, I could sense something. There's no telling what can take place in such a moment. Sometimes I get a feeling as if I can look straight into someone else, as if no boundary exists between the other person and me. She must have felt something like that too, otherwise she wouldn't have walked up to my table or looked at me that way. Or was it just that there weren't any other free seats around? Regardless, I nodded amicably in response to her question of whether a seat was available. I might have even nodded charmingly, since I was still capable of doing that back then.

She sat there and ordered a glass of red wine. She simply sat there and sipped on it. She was such a presence at my table, so completely and totally *there*, that all I could do was stare at her. My gaze must have encouraged her, though I doubt that she needed all that much encouragement. She came right out and said it. She told me that she didn't know where to go for the night. Could I recommend a cheap hotel to her? Of course, I told her she could spend the night at my place. She then squeezed my hand and looked at me as only she could. Yes, and for the next five years, I couldn't get rid of her. After five years, I married her.

What a farce it was back then. She was even abducted on our wedding night. Klaus and Milan really put themselves out on that one. I didn't wait for her to return, since I wasn't willing to play the part of the jealous husband. I just left. They said I vanished, and held it against me.

It was quite good for a while. But the scream in me grew louder and louder. And I drank so I wouldn't hear it any more. I already knew that something was going on inside of her. It often seemed as if she were made of glass, untouchable and terribly sensitive. I extended my tours, but eventually it was winter again, and I found my way back home one day in the gray of dawn. Her room was empty. She had taken everything with her. No note, no explanation.

She called a few weeks later. She said: Darling — Yes, back then that was how we addressed each other — Darling, I'd like a divorce.

If you want a divorce, darling, then let's get a divorce, I said. And that's what we did. It was quite easy and didn't cost anything, since the attorney was a friend of mine.

After the divorce, we got along so well that I actually felt sorry when she left. She called not long after that and said: I need to transfer 170,000 euros for a one-off payment on the new apartment. Will you send me the money, darling? You'll get it back soon, I promise.

I said: Darling, are you crazy? Where am I going to get that kind of money? You know I don't have it.

Then she stopped by my studio. She had lost weight, but anytime you haven't seen your ex-wife for a while, your memories of her change. And when you do see her again, you're shocked. Probably no one is taking care of her. I offered to take her out to eat. She replied that it was nice of me, and she'd be glad to join me, but we had just gotten divorced. As she said that, she looked as if something were bothering her.

And then she came out with it. Of course, she wanted to talk about the payment for her new apartment. She really thought I had the money. If I could have helped her, I would have. She knew that I would've given her my last shirt.

When she finally accepted that I couldn't help her, she grew sad. However, her sadness was sometimes easy to mistake for petulance. She threw a glance at my new picture, half-finished on its easel — I think it was "The Three Witches," from *Macbeth*. She commented tersely: You've done better, darling.

Of course, darling, I retorted. Each of us has done better. Are you sure you don't want to go eat with me?

I'd like to, darling, but you know, there's someone waiting for me.

Where, I asked.

Down in the car, she replied.

Then bring him on up, I said.

Do you really mean that, she wondered.

Sure.

She left and returned with an attractive southern European. This is Nico, she said. Nico comes from Italy. Isn't that true, my little Nico? And she pinched him lasciviously on the cheek. I fetched a bottle of wine.

Did I already mention that her name was Uschi?

TRAVESTY OF LOVE

ELSE FELDMANN
AUSTRIA

Else Feldmann was born in Vienna in 1884, and murdered in 1942 at Sobibor, the Polish extermination camp. She grew up in poverty, briefly attended a teacher training college, and worked in a factory. Starting in 1912, her early literary and journalistic works were published in *Neue Freie Presse* and *Arbeiter-Zeitung*. Feldmann went on to write short stories, novels, plays, and socially critical reports. In 1933, she became a co-founder of the National Federation of Socialist writers, an important part of Viennese literary scene. In 1934, her work was banned by the Nazis, who erased almost all evidence of her work and life.

*Translated by **Rachel Hildebrandt***

I witnessed this tragedy of a woman play itself out one night between eleven o'clock and midnight in a cafe that catered to a "better bourgeois clientele." This would not have been a strange sight in one of the genteel Ring cafes; all of these cafes primarily service the business of love after nightfall.

But in a cafe that was only frequented by the middle class…

Anyway, I want to start from the beginning. A few minutes after eleven, a young woman, hardly more than an oldish girl, entered. Her coat with its fur collar was not missing the requisite fashion flower.

She took off her coat, sat down at a table, ordered a glass of tea.

She sat there in her thin, cheap dress made of artificial silk, a bright little hat on her head. Her unattractive, pointed face with its empty eyes looked gaunt, dilapidated, famished.

She studied all of the tables at which men were sitting with the distinctly timid, sideways glance of the streetwalkers. After a while, she stood up and vanished for a few minutes. When she returned, she looked completely different: her cheeks were pink and white, her lips glowed red, her glances darted forth from eyes underscored in black. Only her shoulders, which jutted out bare and ugly beyond her dress, could not be swapped out. However, she had come up with the idea to ornament herself with a black lace kerchief. Oh, her efforts to attract the men's attention were truly pathetic. For a long time, no one would look at her. Most of the middle class men were well supplied with wives or tarot partners.

The door finally swung open. A black head peered inside. The eyes of the rouged girl sprang to the face, clung there, drew the man inside until he had taken the table next to hers.

You could see that the girl's mood had turned radiant, feverish. Under the pink powder, a flush spread across her skin and down her thin throat, dark red as among those addicted to physical abuse.

The citizens in the cafe began to notice and stare, and something responded in them. Their interest was piqued!

However, the girl was too ugly, and this dampened their eagerness to watch.

It was the man himself. He wore a noxious green woolen scarf crossed across his chest. He was cloaked in a not-very-clean fur car coat and was carrying a crumpled workman's cap in his hand. Perhaps he was unemployed. Celebratory and finding himself in a peevish mood, was he possibly prepared to fritter away the last of his money, regardless of where and with whom?

The girl at the table watched him fixedly and constantly, unconcerned by the other guests. It was a sad gaze, occupied with only one single question: How much will he pay me?

Even the waiters have picked up on this. The head waiter whispers something to the girl at the cash register, who then looks into the mirror in order to observe the nightmarish spectacle from where she is standing: a transaction between two beings in which a body is the commodity. The man with the green scarf looks like a whoremonger. He has an imperious forehead and sturdy, large, coarse hands with red fingers.

He orders a schnaps and then another, calling the waiter, signaling for him. The waiter knows immediately what the guest has ordered, setting another schnaps in front of the girl. She twists her mouth into a distorted smile, drinks.

The waiter moves here and there between the tables, speaking *sotto voce* to the younger wait staff.

The "people's mood" in the cafe takes a turn toward increasing disgust. Everyone seems discontent. A young, plump, vividly painted woman enters, removes her coat, sits down: Tutankhamun blouse, silk stockings, new patent leather shoes. Her gaze immediately starts to wander.

The man with the green scarf stares penetratingly at the Tutankhamun figure. Obviously, a plumper woman pleases him more at the moment.

The plump lady also gazes at the green scarf, strongly drawn to it. The burning eyes from the other table creep forward, slinking like snakes. The creature's entire strength rests in that look. Her behavior is that of a cripple on the street, who begs, who cannot do anything besides lift his eyes pleadingly, plaintively. But he is merciless, searching for somewhere to settle his eyes, somewhere more alluring and tantalizing.

The girl is on the point of despair. Finding herself on unstable ground, she leaves her seat and takes a couple of steps toward the man's table. (For those present, it is supposed to look as if she is asking for the newspaper.) She brushed against him, stood very close to him, striving to entrance him through her proximity, through her perfume. Her rescue came at the last minute. A guest entered. A fat, smug person bristling with financial self-assurance, replete with a flat forehead, tiny eyes, a broad, fleshy neck.

The plump woman had been waiting for him. They retreated further back into a private chamber.

The man with the green scarf ordered hot tea with rum, perhaps it was grog. She just sat there: a tipsily smiling caricature. Midnight was approaching. The bourgeois guests were getting up, heading home, wrapped in their good furs.

In the cafe, it grew still and intimate, like in a small apartment.

You could hear the others' conversations: a heavy heart trembled, corners of a mouth contorted in agony, a flush of shame came and went from a pale face.

These were the newest guests that had entered. They had nothing to do with respectability and middle class mores. Those now trickling in were the liqueur and absinthe drinkers, the occasional and accidental guests from the street.

A youth in peculiar clothing pushed his way to a window seat. He was wearing gauntlet fencing gloves that reached to his elbows. Leather cap with a chin band on his head - pretty, delicate boy, wearing a little make-up. He glanced smilingly over at the man with the green scarf and began to quite openly flirt with him. The girl once again grew feverishly agitated as she saw the fellow, and what he wanted. However, the man made it quite clear that he did not want him.

What a diabolical figure this man with the green scarf was, women and men alike flew at him!

Guests had also noticed this incident. They sat in rapt attention, waiting to see whom he would choose.

The boy drank his coffee, smiled in disappointment, and minced back out the door on his short-trousered legs. The girl exhaled. The startled tension in her face relaxed.

The green man calls: Bill!

She quickly takes her coat down from the rack, slips on her gloves, grasps her handbag, is ready to depart.

But the man has ordered another tea with double rum. Humiliated, she now stays in her seat and waits until he has drunk this. He takes his time, even casting a glance here and there in the satirical paper.

The girl sits patiently and waits. A difficult task for her, to find a man to take her. Part of the night is already past; she has yet to earn anything.

He finally gives her a sign by jerking his chin to the side. She understands. Like a dog, she understands gestures. She is the first one to leave the cafe. Out on the street, she still has to wait for quite a while, until he has finished leisurely skimming the newspaper, slowly buttoning up his coat.

He finally comes…

In Shadow

Andreas Izquierdo
Germany

Born in 1968, **Andreas Izquierdo** is an author and screenplay writer. He has published various works, including the novel *Koenig von Albanien* (2007), for which he received the Sir Walter Scott Prize for the best historical novel of the year, and *Apocalypsia* (2010), which was honored with the Lovelybooks Readers' Award in Silver for the best book of 2010, and was selected as the Book of the Year by Vorablesen.de.

Translated by **Rachel Hildebrandt**

No one even knows that we exist, and this is the only thing that assures our survival. If you knew about us, if we were anything more than an amusing thought flitting across your minds, then you would hunt us down until we were completely wiped out. Each of us lives mutely in your shadows, and it troubles me to think about moving beyond their limits. Not because I'm afraid to do it, since after tonight I won't exist anymore, but because I swore to protect my brothers and sisters. I'm breaking this vow today because I'm no longer who I once was. And what I'm now revealing to you is only a glimpse into one part of the whole, but perhaps it will suffice for you to understand, to understand me.

We adore the big cities and avoid rural retreats. The wealthy neighborhoods don't appeal to us in the least, since we prefer anonymity. A dilapidated high-rise, a prefab building, a concrete hardscape — these make our hearts flutter faster, because these are our homes, the places where the stairs climb forever and the corridors stretch to the right and left of the elevators, like the arms of someone crucified, vanishing into the darkness.

This is where we live.

At least, this is where we sleep. During the day, we live among you: where it's nice, where the heat works, where the television is new, where coasters guard glass-topped tables from unsightly water marks. After all, we appreciate the comforts of life just as much as you do. In the mornings, you go to work and lock your homes, making sure that nobody except yourselves can use them or any of the luxuries contained in them — the ones you don't have time for anyway because you're constantly striving to acquire even more luxuries, none of which you ever really need. And it's while you're toiling away out there that we slip in. We live in your houses and your apartments, using all of the things you think only belong to you.

We wear your shirts, use your toothbrushes, drink from your

glasses, write on your computers, scuff through your homes in your slippers. We read your mail, your diaries. We know all of your photos, your families, your desires and your secrets. We know everything about you, and you have no idea that we exist, because by the time you get home, we're long gone. Your shirts lie in the same piles they had before, your toothbrushes are dry, your computers have been cut off, your mail, your photos, your videos… everything is just the way it was before. You resume the use of your homes, which, until a short while ago, had been ours, as well.

Sometimes, when we can no longer resist the urge, we leave behind little clues. The pencil on your desk whose point is oriented south instead of north. The book that is now tilted the other way on the shelf. The corner of your coverlet that has been turned back. Things like that. Someone told me once that you superstitiously blame washing machines for eating your socks… Have three centuries of Enlightenment and Science really passed you by without a single trace? Sock-eating washing machines? But that's just your nature, and there's nothing you can do about it.

We live among you, in your shadows, but we're not participants in your fate. We're like wolves, ruthless and ravenous, retaining the instincts of our ancestors. Their genes are our genes, and yet we're not like them because some fickle whim of evolution has robbed us for eternity of our freedom. The path to happiness is closed to us forever since we cannot exist without you: you are the keepers of our existence. And regardless of how exhilarating or insipid your life may be, we extract our portion from it in order to live. After all, only that which you fill with life *can* actually live. We are strictly forbidden to intervene in anything or to reveal ourselves, since the survival of our species trumps the survival of the individual. That's our nature, and there's nothing we can do about it.

She changed everything the very moment I entered her shadow. We'll call her Sofia and say that she worked as a secretary in a large office. However, she could also just as easily have been a dental hygienist or an employee in a motor vehicle safety office. Her actual identity is inconsequential. Sofia was not especially pretty or shapely.

She was a little shy, and she lost her will to live relatively quickly, because she no longer believed that she could be successful at anything. She could have used your help, but she was too timid to ask for it. Or perhaps she was smart enough not to, sparing herself at least this one humiliation. She was alone, as she always had been, and as she settled a few more of her affairs with each passing day, she drew me closer to her, from where I was standing in her shadow. Toward the essence of who she was. And that which she was soon found its way to me, infusing my very blood until every fiber of my being pulsed with my awareness that this was what I desired. I began to set aside the cold curiosity with which I extracted my part of life and to fear what would inevitably follow. I sensed it like an animal anticipates an earthquake, and I felt it on that evening when she ran a bath and lit candles, contrary to her normal routine. On the evening that she took a blade with her into the water.

I lingered close to her, waging an internal battle, because her brave fight for your favor had taught me something long ago, something that none of us has ever experienced: compassion. What is strong enough to make you resist your own nature? What shreds you into so many pieces that you can no longer withstand the pain? What besides your own heart can drive you to your doom? And before I was even aware of the boundary I was crossing, I entered her apartment, catching the scent of her blood as it tinged the tub crimson and hearing her breath grow shallow. I made up my mind and stepped out of her shadow. From my perch on the edge of the tub, I reached for her hand and cradled it in mine. Shortly before the end, she opened her eyes, saw me, and smiled. Then she died.

This was the same night I was forced to turn down the path that I had freely chosen, to follow it to its end. To my end. It began with a dream, a warning. This, in and of itself, was unusual since we never have our own dreams. We dream what you dream, since we experience what you experience. In contrast, this dream tumbled through my sleep, until I woke up with a demon on my chest. Chortling, it squeezed my throat harder and harder until I gouged my fingers into its eyes, cracking open its ugly skull and smashing its brain in fury.

Only first then did the pressure on my throat and the weight on my chest abate. As I slowly caught my breath again, I slumped to the floor, disturbed and uncertain about what this was supposed to mean. I didn't go back to sleep that night, and as I crept stealthily from my quarters the next morning, I suddenly knew what had happened: a wolf had moved onto my floor. And whoever or whatever he was, his presence was so terrifying that the pressure around my throat returned. My breath came in short gasps, and I wondered if I would ever be able to escape this constriction. I sank to my knees and struggled to breathe, staring in horror down the hall to the door at the end of it. It was if he could see me, as if he had the ability to pin me down for as long as he wished. Then, in a flash, he released me, and I flew down to the elevator and out of the high-rise.

I was totally baffled because a wolf never occupies another wolf's home. Our instincts are such that we never cross each other's paths, not even inadvertently. It's the same instinct that tells us when it's time to leave your homes, and even if you come home at a strange time of day, you'll never meet a wolf. And now one was living in my home.

I returned that evening, full of dread. Glancing furtively down the corridor, I reached my quarters and searched for my keys. He didn't seem to be home, at least I didn't sense him there. I stole quietly over to his door, closer, closer. Carefully, I placed my hands on the door.

A bolt of lightning surged through my arm, hurling me back into the passage where I landed on my back. I gasped for air as I tried to flee - away from the door, just away from this door! He was at home and had been there the whole time, but I hadn't sensed him until he revealed himself to me. I crawled back to my quarters, panic-stricken. After fumbling with the door, I tore it open, locked it, and crept behind the couch, shivering.

The outside hall light flared on, the light slinking under the crack of the door as a narrow strip. I stared, mesmerized by the glowing rift into another world. I didn't even dare to blink until the shadows shifted, two sets of footsteps that came to a stop in front of my door. They waited there for countless seconds before receding back to where they had come from. Finally, the light went out. The crack under the door lost its magic, and I nervously blinked my rigid eyelids.

I was now dreaming every night, and each of these dreams had something to do with the door at the end of the hall. Time and time again, the fear wrapped itself around my throat, which is why I stopped going to sleep and started staying awake all night. I crept into your beds during the day - I had no other choice - as I searched in anxious silence for some degree of respite.

My time was running out, but I wasn't aware of it doing so. Everything was part of a puzzle, and I could see its separate pieces, although I couldn't make out the entire picture. Perhaps I didn't really want to, existing as I did in a state of numbness and fear. Everything I did fell within the parameters of my daily routine, but my thoughts were overshadowed by what might be coming next. I realize today how insidiously, how seamlessly, one thing flowed into the other. The very moment I began to regain my composure was the one in which the next phase began.

That evening, I returned to my quarters, and for the first time since his arrival, I did not cast even a fleeting glance at the door at the end of the hall. I unlocked my door, stepped inside… All of my instincts went off like warning sirens, my hair bristling in rage, fear, and aggression. He had been in my lodgings, in my space. Before my thoughts had even a chance of settling down, I lunged down the hall and pounded on his door, ready for a fight, ready to abandon my fear and kill him or be killed. He had been in my den, and now I was punching and kicking against his. Yet he refused to open the door, which weathered my outrage and remained bolted.

There was nothing left for me to do but to turn back, exhausted and breathless, to slink away and drown myself in bitter tears of impotence. No wolf ever enters another wolf's lair. That is the law, just like the law that forbids us from revealing ourselves to you. I howled in rage because there was nothing I could do about it or anyone I could turn to. We live alone, we die alone. That is our law, our nature, and there's nothing we can do about it.

It was pointless to wait for him to leave his room in the hope of being able to retaliate and invade his space. His instincts would have tipped him off before I could have even settled on a plan. I left the house the next morning, returning by evening, and the pangs I felt because he was using my life for his own ends, the way I use yours, lessened a little with each passing day, until I reached the point when I couldn't condone it but I could at least live with it. But this too was only a phase, since on the day that I fully accepted this state of affairs, he left behind a clue that I couldn't fail to see. And now it was finally clear where everything was heading, now I understood.

He had moved my computer mouse a few centimeters, just enough so that a single glance could register that it had been used. I immediately booted up the machine, and what I saw was so hopeless, so conclusive, that fear began to thread its cold fingers around my pounding heart. There was nothing I could do but click dazedly through the windows. Everything I had ever written, everything that related to my anonymous, ordinary life in your world, had been deleted: the automatic bill payment contracts for the rent, TV and internet; my chatroom aliases; letters to the insurance and gas companies. It was all just gone! As if I had never existed.

The final phase had started, and it was as if I was plummeting down a deep, black hole. Day after day, something new of mine went missing: a sweater, a toothbrush, a pot, a glass. Since moving beyond your shadow, all of these insignificant things had imperceptibly become elements of identification, elements of an individual life. I owned so very little, but now I was losing everything. I couldn't stop it. All I could do was watch as my apartment dissolved in front of my eyes, in order to be set up again somewhere else: at the end of the hall, behind the door. It was reinventing itself with everything that had once belonged to me.

This morning a pencil vanished, my last possession, and with it the last misguided hope that my dissolution could somehow be prevented. Yet now that everything that once belonged to me is gone and only I remain, I feel better, because they gave me the time to free myself from everything I had once been.

This is how it all ends. Take what I've written to you as the final words of a wolf who stepped out of your shadow to vanish forever. Remember that I had my own place in your life and that I once existed. I don't regret a single thing. I'm going in your stead because I made good on something you should have done. However, I'm leaving with my head held high, and I'm proud of that.

It's time.

I open my door, pull it shut behind me, and gaze down the hall. Light shimmers softly under the crack in the door, and for the first time in a long while, I'm not afraid. I walk to the door, reach for the knob, turn it. It is unlocked.

I step in.

Nothing New Under the Sun

Noga Sklar
Brazil

Noga Sklar was born in Tiberias, Israel, in 1952. She grew up in Belo Horizonte, Minas Gerais, and lived for 30 years in Rio de Janeiro, Brazil. She now lives in Greenville, South Carolina, where she works as a writer and chief-editor with KBR. Noga graduated in architecture from Universidade Santa Úrsula, Rio de Janeiro, but in her youth was better known as a furniture designer and graphic artist. She started to dedicate herself to literature after publishing her first book, in the year 2000 — Fases da Lua, by Editora Madras, republished later by KBR as Eu, xamã — in which she recounts her experiences as a shaman and a New Age activist. It was the beginning of her original style, "self-radiography," better advertised as "autobiographical fiction," a genre she practices still today.

Self-translated by **Noga Sklar**

We were having Thanksgiving dinner at my son's when a friend made the astonishing statement:

"My girlfriend and I never talk about politics."

My mean mind went on to extrapolate, concluding that the couple kept their passionate relationship up and running by avoiding any discussion that could generate a disagreement between the two of them. But what kind of loving intimacy could this be?

"So, Alan, what do they actually talk about?"

"*Uai*, what do you mean? Have you forgotten already? They must talk about their passion, about the stars, about the color of their future children's eyes." (Alan obviously didn't say "uai," which could potentially provoke extreme doubts about the veracity of this report.)

Here at home, as you know, our long-lasting love has been fed mainly by discord, by the hot, passionate tone of our frequent fights about (almost) everything, which, incidentally, has been described by relationship experts as the ideal recipe for a durable marriage. Who knows? For us it has worked so far, and for over ten years.

More recently, however, our efficient "love-war strategy" has been put to a serious test, since after a long dispute over who's right in terms of politics — American politics, at least — I have come to agree with Alan on (almost) everything. And I fear what will come next, as a result of this dreadful general agreement.

And while we are waiting to see where this will take us, I know it's not funny at all, but I can't stop myself from laughing my ass off (Alan encouraged me to write "arse") whenever Obama appears on TV stating that "the biggest enemy we face today is the weather," oops, "climate change." And in the last few days, this has happened every five minutes, especially during the coverage of the summit in Paris.

What's worse, in his global crusade for an all-encompassing lack of sense, having even been labeled by opposition analysts as "pathological," the American luminary has amassed several supporters, including Angela Merkel, the all-powerful European Union leader. As we all know, not so long ago, by deciding to prove her nation as the most charitable of all by opening its doors to hundreds of thousands of refugees (Have you realized that they stopped talking about this subject after the Paris attacks?), Merkel ended up creating a problem she does not know how to solve. I'm not going to share with you the recent comments from a friend who is in Belgium right now, fresh news from the "front," negating part of the media frenzy. As she has told me in confidence, a little shocked, there are rumors that the "refugee camps" in Germany have several features in common with the concen... Shut up, Noga, we're not here to advance hearsay, are we?

Anyway, united world leaders had declared proudly this week in Paris that this climate conference taking place in the City of Lights was the best answer to Isla... oops, shut up again, you cannot call these terrorists by their name today without sounding xenophobic, despite the fact that 99% of the current acts of terror are perpetrated by people who make it obvious, loud and clear, they are acting in the name of... Yes. Him.

You will have to excuse me, but I can't make myself associate these two issues — climate and terrorism — despite the dedication of some patient friends who rush to explain to this intellectually challenged person here that "climate change" causes poverty, insecurity, need, and, as a consequence, terrorism. (Nothing to do with religious fundamentalism and the exploitation of ignorance with meaningless promises, of course.)

Faced with such a logical and direct demonstration of cause and effect, all I can manage to do is go on laughing. It must be a nervous reaction, I don't know. So, an alleged climate change, that may or may not occur in about 100 years, is a more serious challenge to mankind than a gang of soulless brutes who can kill us without notice, anytime, anywhere? Based on a theory that nobody can prove?

It never hurts to remember that the crucible in which this new type of violence (I say "new" because it's based on faith, not on social revolt or something, like the much missed IRA, Baader-Meinhof, and the like, which were previously limited to national aspirations) is being alloyed, is geographically located in a region that has been desert-like and miserable since the times of Harun Al-Rashid, the true Caliph of Baghdad, with his thousand-year old stories of oases and other mental refreshments. Even before that.

All right. I can already envision hundreds of activists, "who mean good," accusing me of being ill-informed, illiterate, etc. Especially now, when, unable to prove that the Earth is really heating up (I'm talking about the temperature, okay?), they decided to change their previous slogan, "global warming" — a famous electoral argument invented many years ago by Al Gore (the said "Al Bore," by the way, lost the election, but never gave up his private, polluting jet) — to "climate change," without specifying exactly what "change" they are talking about. In this way, they will be able to miraculously transmute their cause at any given time to a more convenient "global cooling," which, incidentally, is what Alan has been advocating for years. According to my well-informed husband, the world is actually approaching a mini ice age, mainly due to low solar activity during this period, which, by the way, is not due to careless or criminal human activity, none of that. It is only a natural cycle, as has occurred many times during the life of our beautiful planet.

And as we're into laughing for no reason, I just remembered a Jewish joke, kind of anti-Semitic, but I'm allowed, so there it goes. Consider my option to make the main character Jewish as a goodwill gesture on my part.

So once upon a time there was this opportunistic Jew, who, inspired by stories of space exploration, decided to sell a tourist package to visit the sun.

"But, Moishe," asked the worried prospect, "how's that possible? Isn't it going to be too hot?"

"And what's the problem? We'll go at night."

Right. I won't go into details about the total lack of meaning behind Obama's latest statements because, frankly, although I'm laughing, I'm depressed enough. Our President's main focus is to *pose* as a great global leader, mainly through talking. Incidentally, he seems to believe that simply not calling a horse a horse will stop wild horses from running us over, a shame for the so-called "civilized" world, which seems to feel obliged to embark upon a "liberal politically correct" ship of fools.

As far as I'm concerned, I prefer to end this chronicle with another joke, and you can put two and two together if you wish:

The body parts gathered to choose who among them should be crowned king, or queen, or whatever (today it's always better to leave the gender vague).

The first to make his initial statement was Brain:

"This debate makes no sense at all, as the result is so obvious. From up here, I coordinate everything that happens. I see, I hear, I feel. I interpret and understand, I control our actions and determine our reactions to facts. Therefore, I should be king."

Heart replied immediately:

"Drop that shit, it's too ridiculous. Even if Brain is declared dead I can go on beating, so it is I who deserve to be crowned king. Now, if I decide to stop, there's no life left to pump. How about that?"

And so the meeting went on, with each party defending its platform, some with more energy than others, until you could barely hear, coming from the bottom, a little tiny voice:

"You can stop all this talk right this second! There is no doubt that I should be made the king of the body!"

Protest came in unison. What power could that small, insignificant body part have? It was often dirty, stinky, acting imposingly and uncontrolled. Its mere name is considered bad taste among educated folks.

"Okay, then. I'll shut myself down for a few days and after that we can decide. Agreed?"

And so it was done. After a couple of weeks, the body reunited and Arse was unanimously declared king.

I don't need to remind you that, in the privacy of our unconfessed brilliant thoughts, we probably prefer to see this whole violence, whose name we cannot say, as an annoying threat emerging from the world's asshole, oops, sorry.

THE END [1]

LUCIO ROBERTO MARZAGÃO
BRAZIL

1 An excerpt from *Freud and His Long Journey into Death*, KBR, 2012.

Lúcio Roberto Marzagão has a Master's Degree in Philosophy from UFMG (Minas Gerais, Brazil), where he has been an Associate Professor for thirty years. Presently he is a teacher at the *Lato Sensu* Postgraduate Program in Psychoanalytic Theory at UFMG. He also published *Psicanálise e Pragmática*, in 1966, and the 2nd edition of *Psicanálise e Literatura* with KBR in 2012.

*Translated by **A.H. Lin***

I awoke and immediately remembered what I wrote in what I assumed would be my last letter to Princess Marie: "A small island of pain floating on an ocean of indifference." Some months later, I cannot make the same statement. The small island has become a continent. It has spread out in concentric circles and invaded every corner of my body. My body is a continent surrounded by people's attention. Their compassionate expressions display well-meaning concern. I live at the painful division between my decrepit body, progressively less responsive, failing body and my mind, still attentive and thoughtful. Feeling like a stranger in my own body, I am at the end; but I know that in these last moments, I will not shrink in fear from death. During my life, I sought consistency, at the same time delighting in inevitable change. When I talked with Lou and Rilke, I sometimes argued that the true beauty of life resides in the constant change of the tree's clothing with each season. Through the window, I can see that the Gregorian calendar prevails outside: Autumn is beginning. But inside this room I have no doubt that my winter approaches.

The pain is indescribable. It comes as a great irony: All my life I professed that the true liberation of the soul comes from transforming pains, feelings, and affects into words; but now that it is my turn, I can't manage to focus my attention. The pain has claimed everything for itself, everything.

Without exception, everyone in the house was exhausted. I had to submit to many different, humiliating medical procedures. But, as if there were a tacit agreement among us all, one moment we would deny the gravity of the illness and laugh together; at the next moment, our smiles came framed by dejection. I saved my tearful wails of sadness for sleepless early mornings. During my life, I have cried very few times, but when Sophie and my grandson left, the pain of loss was truly beyond my capacity to endure.

Freud and Sophie.

I hope that if I kept my eyes closed, the pain would diminish as it does when I hold still. It has become increasingly difficult to speak. Few of them can make sense of my sighs or the words I carefully form with swollen, sore lips. Paula manages to understand, especially when I ask for something simple. At times, Annerl can make out my comments. Martha watches closely with her arms crossed over her heart to contain her racing heartbeat, but she comprehends very little of what I say. Minna's illness prevents her from leaving her bedroom on the floor above, but she sends messages. Max — for many years my physician and now my confidante — has returned from the United States and moved to Maresfield Gardens. He now stands at my headboard, looking from side to side like a soldier guarding an important place against an imaginary enemy.

"Guten Morgen, Herr Professor, Entschuldigung." With these cheerful words, my beloved Paula enters the room. Her discerning eyes scan my bed and debilitated body. She approaches. Almost whispering, I tell her that we no longer have to speak in German. A year has passed since we received an unforgettable reception bordering on veneration. As for the deference to me as a professor, I insist she never again address me this way. Austria and its rulers would not permit it. And breakfast can wait. I no longer care about time. I have learned to pay attention to details, and I know that some details, like eating, for example, are now irrelevant.

Time always ordered my activities. Now, I busy myself with self-observation. I respond, "Hello, Miss Paula!" With both of her legs leaning against my bed, she draws near my head, adjusts my pillow, pulls up a chair, and sits close to my face. Holding a bowl with hot steaming broth, she delicately lifts my head and, without speaking, fills the spoon. I accept the soup, but can't recognize the taste of the broth. I wave the spoon to say thank you and pretend that I taste the broth. In truth, I like her taking care of me.

During the final days, I notice that my breathing had become progressively more labored. I no longer have control of my sphincters — a humiliating development that mimics my father's final suffering. Max has told me that my blood sugar level is no longer the same, so on top of everything else, I am absorbing food slowly. The broth feels hot in my mouth, and when I swallow, it energizes me. With effort, I turn to young Paula's compassionate face. I try to smile, wanting the smile to communicate my gratitude. Paula is part of my family. It took some time for the other women — Martha, Anna, and Minna — to accept her ways; but now she has earned everyone's admiration, even that of friends and colleagues living in Europe and the United States.

With open eyes, I watch Annerl enter. As always, she seems to be restless. She inspects the room as if she were a supervisor, looking for something out of place. When she looks me in the eye, I understand that she has been waiting for my pain to pass. She greets me affectionately, asks about my sleep; and, when I don't respond, she understands immediately. She looks at Paula inquisitively, and with her look, Paula answers that everything is good. Paula leaves the room, taking the bowl.

"Hello, daughter. Did you sleep well?"

"Yes, father, but I can't get accustomed to the noise from Finchley Road. The busses never sleep. Was the broth good? I'm sure you would prefer some eggs, tartar sauce, ham, and vanilla ice cream, but you can't eat ice cream in the morning, and liquid foods will be more easily absorbed. When you're better, we will have ham and toast."

We look at each other and understand that this day will never come.

I look at Anna and, in a weak voice, tell her that I would like to ask a favor.

"Sure, Papa. What is it?"

"I should respond to a friend's letter. I want to dictate it. Would that be possible?"

"A letter? Now is not the best time…"

"Well, Annerl, when it comes to a friend, I always respond to letters. It is for Albrecht Schaeffer, a German writer who wrote to me about mythology and mysticism, and translated Oscar Wilde, Diderot, and Verlaine into German. He is also moving to the United States."

"Very well, Papa, dictate it."

"Thank you."

Dear Mr. Schaeffer,

What an unexpected and welcomed letter! I have thought of my poet often in recent times, empty in some ways, asking myself how these wildly turbulent recent events in your birthplace have affected you! It brought me great pleasure to know that what I feared did not happen and that you found a precious partner in your wife.

You would not be pleased to hear everything I could tell you about myself, but I am eighty-three years old. Therefore, the fact is my time has passed, and nothing remains for me to do except to follow the advice of your poem: Hope, Hope.

Cordially yours,

"Annerl, put this letter in the mail, today, if possible."

The doorbell rings, and Anna immediately explains that it might be Professor Ernest Jones, who had said yesterday that he would make a quick visit before seeing his patients. Instead, the barber enters the bedroom and begins to sharpen his razor, while talking about the war and England's hesitation to enter the conflict.

"Cowardice," he says.

Then he mechanically spreads the foam on my face, and I see that when he scrapes the right side of my face, he does it very slowly and cautiously, with special care to the surgical scars. I note, too, that he holds his breath while standing close to my face. As a matter of fact, everyone does that, including my dog, which keeps moving further and further from my bed... After a few minutes, the barber hurries out and says good-bye, explaining that his schedule is full of appointments.

I am sitting in a chaise-longue on the deck of a ship, smoking, and watching the limitless ocean... I am afraid and at the same time feel that I am ready to achieve glory and recognition... Jung and Ferenczi draw close... They say something I cannot understand... Jung moves in front of me and impedes my view of the water and the horizon... I move my head, and he moves again, still in front of me... I am irritated... I wake up.

Freud and Ferenczi in 1917.

Once again, the doorbell interrupts my torpor. After a few minutes, Ernest and Anna enter the room. He wears a dark suit and tie, elegant as always, and greets me in a strong, optimistic voice. I greet Jones, slowly lifting my arms in a sign of discouragement. He takes a seat in the same chair Paula had used a few minutes before and begins to talk about the British Psychoanalytic Society. I silently listen to his worry about the exile of the psychoanalysts from the continent, whether forced or voluntary. Many are Jews, and the British psychoanalysts are feeling threatened. Without speaking, I wonder if Jones might be anti-Semitic. *I cannot interpret his statement in this way. My reception by the English suggests the opposite,* I think. Knowing that Ernest does not want to hear my opinion, I make an ambiguous gesture, agreeing with his words, and I allow drowsiness to overtake me once more. This will be Jones' last visit. I have become profoundly averse to political problems of any sort. I am only concerned with my daughter's professional future and with a solution to her problems with Mrs. Klein. I never know if my daily sleep reduces my fatigue or makes it worse.

Marie Bonaparte, Melanie Klein, Anna Freud, and Ernest Jones.
Photo Edward Bibring.

After some time, I open my eyes. The bedroom is empty. My gaze passes over the bookcase, a small four-step ladder that has served me throughout my entire life, the divan, and an easy chair, all instruments of work; there among them, I recall laments, cries, and laughter. The hearth is dark, and I think that I will never again see it lit and crackling. Some of the books, my daily companions, are worn from constant use. Others wait their turn. The antiques... a lot of pain... everything has a story, evidence of my interest in archeology and other sciences, and most were given me by friends and colleagues. The value of the pieces is incalculable to me; as a collection, it is worth little. I look at each of them and visualize the person who gave me every piece, the occasion, and what the object means. In the cupboard which houses the collection, a Greco-Roman vase stands out — a present from Princess Marie Bonaparte — a vase which was used to hold wine or honey and decorated by figures of people in ritual offerings. It is my favorite piece. I am interested in the archeological value of the pieces, but at that moment, they reveal other meanings, principally the artistic. Finally, I look at the writing desk, where I have written about discoveries concerning the soul, discoveries which threatened people. At times, I paid dearly for that small piece of luck.

Everyone around me knows, and remains cautiously silent about my approaching death, drawing closer with each moment. The movements around me grow increasingly theatrical. I act, and my small audience always responds as expected. I protect myself from this unpleasantness by sleeping or pretending to sleep, and everyone pretends to believe I am sleeping.

Now constantly silenced by the pain, I reflect over the past and the future of the science which I have conceived. Will posterity think of my work as literature or science? Will I be compared to Shakespeare or to Darwin?

I realize that it is September 19. On this day, especially in Italy, the Catholic church celebrates St. Gennaro, a martyr buried in Naples whose blood is preserved in small bottles and liquefies on this day every year. Despite my lack of faith, on certain occasions I used St.

Gennaro and a poem by Virgil to argue with a skeptical colleague about the undeniable existence of the Unconscious. On one such occasion, I asked my friend to recite the poem, and he forgot the word, *aliquis.* I told him that his forgetting was not random, but affected. Actually I am certain that psychoanalysis will not be accepted by force of argument, but rather by the patient's life experience. I consider the rest of the debate useless and tiring.

Nostalgic for the recent past, I reminisce about one time when I walked slowly down the street at Maresfield Gardens to the avenue that had a metro station. Nearby was a cigar store, where the proprietor knew of my routine and my addiction. When he saw me approaching, he waved, smiled, and spoke in slow, understandable English. He immediately offered me a box of cigars. I paid and thanked him, as if it were a present. On the way back, I watched the movement of cars and people; I responded mechanically to the greetings of those I knew and those I didn't. I arrived home, lit a cigar and from time to time gazed at it at arm's length, and lost myself in the fragrant smoke. Since the age of twenty-four, cigars have been my constant companions, as much as the books. Besides helping me work, they have helped me concentrate. One time, I told my grandson, Harry, that I couldn't understand the fact that he didn't smoke, since that was my greatest and cheapest entertainment. I smoked progressively less, and eventually I regularly smoked around twenty cigars per day. The scene during the Society meetings was comical. Everyone there held a cigar, as they talked incessantly about psychoanalytic theory. People say that on one occasion, when faced with a colleague's insistence about the psychological meaning of a cigar, I told him that at times a cigar is only a cigar! When someone reminds me of this, I respond that I don't remember having written or said anything like that.

I puff and return to rereading *Moses and Monotheism*. I think about death: A human being spends a good part of his life trying to deny death, his own or the deaths of the people he loves. Without a doubt, writing books or creating works of art are among the activities that facilitate mourning our losses. With shocking ingenuousness, children ask their mothers, "When you die, should I do... [this or that]? Well, everyone knows the phrase, "*si vis pace, para bellum.*" *(If you seek peace, prepare for war).* I prefer, "*si vis vitam, para mortem*" *(If you want to live, prepare for death).*

I see Max's face, distressed and hurried. Two weeks ago, more specifically, on September 3, a Sunday, England declared war on Germany. Max was in the garden where I was sunning myself and reading journals. He told me that the sirens were not a simple training exercise and moved me to the office on the ground floor as a precaution. So, there I was, looking at furniture, my collected objects. I remembered Shaw saying, "Don't try to live forever. It can't be done!"

When with eyes closed, I sense that no one is in the room, I surrender myself to daydreams and digressions. One more time, my increasingly cloudy consciousness returns to those holidays that I enjoyed on Austria's border with Italy, in the Dolomite Mountains in San Martino de Castrozza. As I've noted already, I was having a conversation with my friends Lou Andreas-Salomé and Rilke. They complained about the transitory nature of life, and I argued that the beauty of life derived precisely from the changes, the cycles, and the overcoming of difficulties. And once more, I am here, fighting against death, and for the second time in the same day, remembering this one episode.

The sound made by a troop of soldiers marching down the road makes me think about war. I continued fighting in Vienna for dozens of years, suffering all the prejudices, whether expressed openly subtly. I was analyzing colleagues and friends coming from different countries and wanted to stay on the Berggasse at whatever price. I didn't believe that the Nazis would arrive at my door. After Annerl was arrested by the Gestapo, I felt defeated. Now I have been living in London for a year. My colleagues and my sisters almost certainly will be killed by Hitler. Forgive me. I recognize, finally, that if I had stayed in Vienna, psychoanalysis would have disappeared — it would have come at the hands of the Nazis, or the hands of the communists who certainly will take power. The decision to move to London, while difficult, saved not only the lives of those I love, but also allowed psychoanalytic theory a chance to survive and spread throughout the world. I never disguised my antipathy for the *modus vivendi* of the Americans, but their capacity to transform everything they put their hands on into an object to consume offered my discoveries a chance to gain strength and recognition. They, those Americans, are a type of modern-day Midas.

Rilke and Lou Andreas-Salomé in 1897, on the porch of the Andreas family summer home.

From my bed, I follow the movement of the sun. Night is falling. At night, I feel more apprehensive. I feel little longing for Martha, more for Annerl and Paula. The pain grows, and my daydreams lose all logic. The mosquito netting protects me from the flies but partially obstructs my view of the road. The light dims and lets the twilight enter.

Paula enters still smiling, greets me, now in English, and offers me vegetable soup. I note that despite all her efforts, she keeps back from my lacerated face. She insists on feeding me; and when Annerl enters, I have a spoon in my mouth and am unable to greet her.

After dinner, they both leave, and I turn my attention to the antiques, my old and good gods, to the origin of religions — a theme that never abandons me. Greek gods, Roman or Egyptian — all lined up in a row, observing my suffering. I know I am dying. But how does one defeat death? I can't, except by writing books, though one doesn't know if they will be read in the future. I remember that Nazi phrase that at times has been used against my contributions and those of other Jewish writers: "We are against the glorification of the instincts; we want to restore the nobility of the human soul; thus, we burn the books of Sigmund Freud." I thought that, surely there has been some progress since the burning of witches in the Middle Ages: Now they content themselves with burning books.

It is night, and I see someone enter the bedroom. I close my eyes and pretend to nap; at the same time, I ask, both in fear and happiness, "*More visits?*"

SUNDAY[2]

ANGELA DUTRA DE MENEZES
BRAZIL

2 An excerpt from *All the Days in the Week*, KBR, 2012.

Angela Dutra de Menezes is a Brazilian writer and journalist. She was born in Rio de Janeiro, and is now living in Porto, Portugal. She worked at *O Globo* and on the weekly magazine *Veja*. She wrote *A Thousand Years Minus Fifty* (1995), *Saint Sofia* (1997) — considered in Spain one of the 5 best novels of the year 1997 — *The Other Side of the Picture* (1998) and *The Book of Apocalypses according to a Witness* (2001). In 2000, she published the collection of essays *The Portuguese that gave Us Birth* — one of the 10 best books of the year according to *O Globo*. *All the Days of the Week* is her first book of short stories and her first book translated into English.

Translated by **Fal Azevedo**

Since his youth, when he used to dream of flying saucer crew members dictating messages to him in incomprehensible languages, Edmundo Santos Fogaça has dedicated all his free time to the study of Ufology. In his accounting office, he accumulated piles and piles of documented evidence of the aliens' invasion of the serene routine of our humble planet. From analyzed photographs — of which there was no chance of forgery, as confirmed by the security seal affixed by NASA to the recorded tapes of the incomprehensible language — identified, but not decoded, though Fogaça had researched thousands of publications in countless libraries.

Finally, his tireless efforts were gloriously rewarded. It was a language of the Orion family, specifically of the Lacteous branch — information that he had found in an old dictionary edited in the extinct Soviet Union, one of the triumphs of the Galactic infiltration; Stalin himself was actually a disguised alien, of noble origin, by the way. Fogaça made sure to emphasize that Stalin had been born of the Sagittarius line, under the star *Eta Carinae*, in the Nebula of the same name.

"Wow, he must have had trouble sending a letter to his mother," joked one of his friends, which caused the end of the friendship. Edmundo Santos Fogaça could never accept playful comments regarding such an important subject. After insulting the mediocre ex-friend, who could only see the obvious, Fogaça added:

"Poor terrestrial man, you are nothing but an amoeba. You need to learn how to listen, as Jesus taught. He was an alien ahead of his times, worshipped and adored, and nobody dared to doubt or analyze his powers, which were miraculous gifts from the peoples of the universe. If you studied a little before uttering idiocies you would know that Stalin belonged to a race that has wandered space for millennia, looking for new harbors, no longer able to deal with the excess of their population."

The unshakeable faith in alien civilizations, all with the fixed objective of conquering the Earth, forced him to remove himself from the daily habits of normal people — going to the beach or to the cinema, reading, dancing, and listening to music, for instance. Besides other Ufologists, Fogaça had no friends. His life was limited to his work as a freelance accountant and the planetary-metaphysical research. There was no detail about flying saucers, humanoids, or aliens living among us in disguise — learning our ways to eventually conquer us — which he did not know about. In spite of the disbelief of some of his peers, Fogaça had even met the Varginha Alien himself, having conversed with him several times — telepathically, of course. Fogaça had never learned Lacteous-Oranian, and the Varginha Alien could not speak Portuguese, although Fogaça could have sworn that, after tasting the traditional "*doce de leite*"[3] from Minas Gerais, the alien was unable to look at a cow without saying, "*Trem bão, sô.*"[4]

Following a well-organized and boring routine, Fogaça waited for Sundays with obvious emotion. Year after year, just after sunrise, he would travel from Rio to Petropolis, a city in the mountains. There, on the top of the Retiro Hill, there was a landing field for alien ships, where he would wait for 24 hours, waiting for a miracle — who knows, they might come to abduct him! Fogaça would bet his entire Ramil fortune[5] that an extraordinarily large mother ship travelled around Earth, and that she would soon release her daughter ships to save those who believed in a larger life, a life beautiful enough to go beyond this shitty little planet, lost in the universe, to escape the impending apocalypse. Those who knew better would say that only terrestrial scum could cultivate the vanity of seeing their world as the center of the universe. It was about that subject and other topics — invariably, cosmonautic gossip — that Fogaça and the other regular visitors of the landing field would speak, while they waited for a *Close Encounter of the Third Kind* — visualizing flesh and bone (or whatever material they were made of) aliens, face to face. A *Close Encounter of*

---

3 Typical dessert from the State of Minas Gerais, made with milk and sugar.
4 Popular expression in Minas Gerais meaning, "This is awesome."
5 Currency used in Vulcano, a planet hidden by the Mercury orbit and inhabited by humanoids with asbestos bodies.

the Third Kind seemed to be a dream — it never happened. However, on one chilly night, Fogaça and two friends had the honor and privilege of hearing the conversation between an alien couple. According to the insiders, the trio had made the equally rare *Close Encounter of the Second Kind*, a true apotheosis. Unfortunately, the three men could not understand what the couple said, or figure out how they had appeared on the hill. For hours, they searched the splendid blue of the winter night, but there was not one single spaceship in the sky. Suddenly, out of nowhere, the aliens appeared. The evidence of this occurrence — Fogaça took pictures of them and recorded their conversation — generated months of discussions and a thesis published in the famous London newspaper *New Age News.*

Signed by Edmundo dos Santos Fogaça, the revolutionary discovery, documented in beautiful photographs, argued in a meretricious narrative that alien beings were made of human matter, and that — surprise! — the male had had something similar to the flu — between grunts, he sniffed and panted until he fell, almost breathless, on top of his female companion, who rocked him gently until he could stand up again. As Fogaça skillfully wrote in his conclusion to the article, through the immeasurable competence of Brazilian Ufologists, they had obtained proof of the soul that lived inside those strange bodies — a proof they had been searching for centuries: "[…] there is no reason to fear our alien brothers, they have the feelings of superior spirits. I have seen it with my own eyes, the female was extremely tender."

Even with the sensation caused in the international esoteric communities — East and West inviting Fogaça, the new expert in interplanetary metaphysics, to attend debates and conferences — the best result of this spectacular field research was his marriage to a shop assistant who worked in the photo shop where he had the sensational films developed. A beautiful, charming brunette, Magda da Conceição, had been taken aback when she looked at the photos — *well, well, who could have imagined?* The moment Fogaça showed up to pick up the photos, she shook her shoulders, flashing the sure smile of those who have just hit their target:

"So! What a surprise, Mr. Fogaça! Have you given up on the aliens? That was unexpected, you and your attitude, with a weak spot for dirty pictures…"

Edmundo Santos Fogaça did not waste his time with ignorant people who were incapable of seeing the beauty in the occult. Explain to that poor girl the scientific importance of what she had in her hands? Imagine that. Despite his irritation with such stupidity — the girl could see sex in the most serious discovery ever made by mankind — something powerful kept him chained to the photo shop. Standing before Magda, he analyzed every angle of the pioneer work, solemnly ignoring the curious comments:

"My God, I have never done anything like this! Jesus, Mr. Fogaça, are you perverted? Look, what a well-endowed alien! Are you going to sell the pictures to porn sites?"

The scientific soul of Edmundo Santos Fogaça could not take the offense. He looked at the shop assistant, ready to confront her; to call the manager and ask that she be fired immediately. But he ended up drowning in the waves of her eyes, two emerald drops, shining with mischief, with life, with intent. To make the story short, they were married within the year — both madly in love. She knew well her husband's manias, but was willing to accept them. She did not believe any of the foolish theories researched by Fogaça, but the man was worthy. He was kind, generous, sweet and funny, and honored his name by being the perfect lover. On his part, he accepted the total absence of neurons in his wife's head. In his opinion, Magda was just like the majority of terrestrials — nothing but a fool who could see only what was before her eyes. Theirs was, ideologically and philosophically, the perfect marriage; the spouses knew each other's flaws, and that match could never fail.

And indeed, it did not fail. Madga brought some joy to the black-and-white life of the star accountant. She organized his papers, the boxes and boxes of photos and documents about UFOs, abductions and creepy stories. To lighten up the atmosphere of the office, which was heavy and suffocating because of all those mysteries, she had set up a file system, correlating incidents according to the events that mankind was going through when they had occurred.

That was how the "Alien DOI-CODI"[6] came to be a common visitor during the 1970's. The Pelé abduction had happened in 1958. Magda called Saddam a 2003 alien of unpredictable habits — he came and went without logic — a name that her husband's friends, as nuts as he was, immediately adopted.

"Sorry, I'm late, traffic problems. Has Saddam showed up?"

"Not yet. But the spaceship flew by twice."

Not even his Close Encounter of the Second Kind, for which Fogaça was honored as a *Scientist of Super and Sublunary Astrophysics*, escaped Magda's irony. Laughing, she named the event "Fellatio." The envelope with the evidence and the souvenirs from the event that had shaken modern thinking had actually been named after this vulgar expression, and Fogaça was angered. After much debate, they chose a more suitable word, appropriate to the importance of the famous researcher. Deep inside, Fogaça liked Magda's reckless lightness — if she did not believe, at least she was sincere and had a good sense of humor. God forbid his own wife should make fun of him behind his back.

Until she became pregnant with their first child (a boy they named Hubble, after the telescope), Magda always accompanied Fogaça on the weekly trips to the landing field in Petropolis. She took fruit, cans of beer, boiled eggs — changing the study meeting into a picnic. When Asdrubal Penaforte, a retired doctor who was the leader of the Ufologists, complained about the heresy — *if that went on, the research meeting would end up as a party* — Magda explained:

"First of all, Dr. Asdrubal, if the aliens come, we must welcome them with kindness, showing them we are friends. Besides, I don't think they will take long. I think they will come from one of the hundred extra-solar planets we have evidence of. I personally think our contact will be made with someone from HD 209458B, which orbits the star HD 209458, very similar to the sun and only 150 light years away from the Earth. You know that HD 209458B is located in the Pegasus constellation, don't you?"

Thank God, Saddam had not finished his landing maneuvers

6 Investigation Government Department during the military dictatorship in Brazil.

yet and had escaped the commotion. Everyone was flabbergasted, including Fogaça. Saddam would also be affected by this sudden, weird knowledge exhibited by Magda. Not even Asdrubal's medicine would have saved the alien, an organism that was not fond of oxygen, if he had gone into shock at these extraordinary words of the young Mrs. Fogaça, a beautiful homemaker, whom nobody took seriously. When she stopped talking, Magda saw her husband's pride and the surprised expression on the others' faces. From that day on, they started to consider her one of them. But there were those who believed there was more to her — *Magda was actually an alien.*

Magda took advantage of that fact and had a lot of fun. Every now and then, without warning, she said something that would cause a fuss. Fogaça was having a ball; he knew she was just joking, but the rest of the gang was breathless — how could a simple girl, who was nothing more than a shop assistant before she married Fogaça, know so many details about noble interstellar protocol? On the next Sunday, without asking Fogaça's permission, a group decided to force her to explain the source of that knowledge. She did not think twice:

"Fogaça teaches me. Come on, I ask, he answers. You seem to forget that my husband is a genius, respected all over the world — in all worlds. I know, for instance, that Saddam is not coming today. The core of his planet was severely reduced, and this has made life impossible. Poor Saddam, he lived in an inhabitable star system. As you surely are aware, planets evaporate when they are less than seven million kilometers away from a star. The radiation disperses hydrogen, and there isn't a single planetary mass that can survive a leak of 60 miles per second. Would anyone like a sandwich, a piece of cake?"

And so it was. The excess of knowledge defined Magda, who undoubtedly belonged to the class of the *sent ones*, the inquisitors concluded. To explain further, though Magda was unaware of the fact, she was part of an *Advanced Order* — groups from other spheres, transported to Earth to understand it and conquer it. Fogaça's wife, the geniuses of the group quickly concluded, did not belong to the human race. It actually made sense. Fogaça, the best among the best, had probably married the great-granddaughter of Stalin, a deserved award for such an expert on UFOs and aliens.

"*Habemus* alien," said Dr. Asdrubal, looking at Magda's ass. *What an ass*, he thought. I*t is worth waiting for others like that, so round, to fall from the sky, right on top of his head.*

When she heard the comments, Magda did not hesitate, she started to learn Russian. On Sundays, when she arrived at the landing field, she greeted the friends in an offhanded manner:

"*Dóbray útra*. I mean, good morning."

And she went on her way smiling, indifferent to the surprise she caused with her linguistic slip. As they started to forget her, Saddam would return to the center of the debate — *could he have vaporized just like his planet?* Magda would then say something in Russian, and they would look at her with astonished interest again. She repeated so many "*spaassiba*" — when she meant thank you; so many "*des vidania*" — to say goodbye — and "*pajalsta*" — as a sign of gratitude, that one fine day Asdrubal made an announcement. He said that the Brazilian Ufology Society,[7] during a secret meeting in which he had had the honor of participating, representing Petropolis and the deceased Saddam, had decided that Magda should be the subject of a rigorous study, due to her surprising knowledge of the cosmos and her alarming command of the Soviet language. Magda's green eyes became larger — she made an innocent face and protested:

"*Ya ni gavariu pa Russki*. I mean, I can't speak Russian."

Fogaça, the scientist, a brilliant and devout man who had dedicated his life to the search for the wanderers of the sky, reacted like any hot-blooded South-American macho man:

"Let's not mix friendship with business. She's my wife, and nobody touches her, end of story!"

Divine Providence never fails. Before Fogaça had the chance to argue with his old friends, and before disorder reigned among the researchers, Magda got pregnant and stopped accompanying her husband on the Sunday trips. She said that the smell of space-

---

7 Non-profit entity, with the right of vote in the Space Galactic Confederation.

ship fuel made her morning sickness worse. Fogaça almost died laughing.

"You're incorrigible. Do you think I believe that? But it's a good excuse."

To be fair, Magda's absence reduced the charm of the vigils in Petropolis. No more coffee; no more sandwiches; no more cakes, sweets and fruit; and especially, no more joy — for Magda could always make a funny comment out of the blue. The hours seemed to take longer to pass. Even the aliens showed their discontent, and started to come less and less often. Sometimes a spaceship gave signs of life and the Ufologists went crazy. They forgot about Magda and engaged in exciting discussions: who the aliens were; where they came from; if they finally would dare to make direct contact.

Meanwhile, in Rio, Magda behaved in a irreprehensible manner. She woke up late; watched television; spent the whole day alone. The neighbors talked about how lucky Fogaça was, that raving mad lunatic. The flying saucer hunter who went after aliens with a butterfly net had married a young woman who was honorable, beautiful and friendly. "She is too good for him," said the building administrator, with an ironic tone. She disliked Fogaça and her feelings were reciprocated — he hated her.

But it was the building administrator who helped Magda when Hubble decided to be born on a Sunday. When he came back home on Monday, with lots of stories to tell — they had almost had another *Encounter of the Second Kind* but the aliens were scared off by Asdrubal's sneezing — Fogaça bumped right into the angry lady, who was waiting for him at the door:

"What a shame, Mr. Fogaça! While you were playing hide and seek with the aliens, your beautiful wife gave birth to a boy. They are both very well, thanks to God and to me, who took her to the hospital in time. Now, try to get some sense, because you're an adult and you have a son to raise."

After Hubble's birth, the routine changed. Too busy with the little heir, Magda never returned to the landing field again and lost interest in Fogaça's files. But one day, hearing him talk about the scare they had had with a spaceship that had almost crashed into the Rio-Petropolis motorway, she seemed to relive the old times. She blinked those green eyes and asked her husband to tell her about the episode in detail.

In the hope of seeing his wife keeping him company again and coloring his Sundays with her spirit, Fogaça exaggerated the details of the golden lights of the spaceship, its maneuvers in trying to land with the grace of a bird, until the dramatic moment when the UFO shook, recovered its elegance, stabilized, and disappeared. Feigning indifference, Magda declared:

"That was not a spaceship, Fogaça. What you are describing is a flying drag queen, falling from her high heels."

That was the last involvement Magda ever had in her husband's research. From that day on, when she was not pregnant, she was breastfeeding. She only remembered the aliens when the children were born and Fogaça gave them preposterous names, Hubble, Zeta Grey and Moth: three green-eyed boys, Magda's green eyes, emerald waves with magnetic attraction. Despite the distance from his wife, who had become more and more disconnected from the alien business, Fogaça was a happy man. He never noticed Magda's irritation with the lack of money, for he had abandoned his accountancy office — he lived exclusively to track and search the ends of the nebulas. He could only see the mess he was in one Monday, when he returned from Petropolis and found a note on the table:

On Sunday, the ships are coming to the planet Earth. I will go with the children. One day, perhaps I will return to this world. Be happy. Magda.

Fogaça was desperate. He could never forgive himself for having stopped Asdrubal from studying the woman — all that grace, those eyes, her strong and honest attitude. Only Fogaça, the famous scientist, had not noticed that his wife was an alien in disguise.

He never had the courage to tell the truth to the Ufologists in Petropolis; he had spent the last ten years having a *Close Encounter of the Third Kind*. No human being had ever accomplished that before, and Fogaça, as any other husband, had not seen the miracle. Tortured by guilt, he kept his vigil at the landing field — he did not stop to rest for one second, always waiting for his family.

Meanwhile, in Vitória da Conquista, a city in the interior of Bahia, Magda and the three boys were living with the building administrator's son, a pragmatic bank clerk who could only see the moon, the sun, and the stars in the sky — as well as airliners at times. She was happier now. With Fogaça at her side, her fear had become panic — his friends from Petropolis had come dangerously close.

Yes, she was an alien. Not from *Carinae*, but from Orion. Her name was Artemis — and her beautiful green eyes were multimedia instruments that photographed and filed every human detail. Then, in a mere blink, the data was zipped and sent in Lacteous-Oranian via wireless internet to her home planet.

With Magda's help, Earth would soon belong to another civilization.

Samba-Canção[8]

Eduardo Borsato
Brazil

8 An excerpt from *Samba-Canção*, KBR, 2012. Literally, "Samba Song" — a sad and romantic old musical genre; but it is also a *double entendre*, referring to old-fashioned long briefs worn by Brazilian men.

Eduardo Borsato is a playwright, novelist, and short story author. He has worked as a ghostwriter and as a television scriptwriter for TV Globo, where he adapted soap opera texts for books and pocket books. For ten years, he was the editor of newsletters and neighborhood newspapers. A prolific writer, he has published nine books with KBR, including novels, plays and short stories.

*Translated by **A.H. Lin***

He could never accept Isabel's wedding. The most coveted girl in Belisario dos Santos High School, candidate for Miss Campo Grande — not elected due to the quintessential stupidity of the judges — was always flirting with him. In just a short leap, they were dating.

"He is the luckiest guy in the world!" grumbled his classmates, purple with envy.

Then she suddenly met Machado. They married in six months. Passions boiling, she didn't even finish her studies.

"She is going to realize she made a big mistake. Young, pretty, highly doable — *you have no idea* what happened!"

But feeling the pain of the spurned lover, he knew very well that nothing had happened, except...

"What was Machado's secret? What?"

The young widow

"Nothing," she responded. "If you are going to keep asking this, you can stop calling me."

"There must be something. There must."

"Did you hear me? Rehashing. I'm going to hang up."

"Don't do it. Don't..."

Her tribulations appeared to have no end. After the wedding, she and Machado had moved to Bangu. He was a wholesaler on the grocery-and-liquor-store circuit — the worst wholesaler there was, by the way.

"He went into bankruptcy. It put her in a very bad position," said Carvalhinho, the lawyer, in confidence. And, whispering into his ear, he added, "It was Machado's total incompetence. A huge loss. That's why he died."

Isabel, the widow, returned to Campo Grande.

"Living from hand to mouth. She rents an apartment. Without two pennies to rub together. She works to pay the bills," continued Carvalhinho.

And, wetting his lips, "But she's still hot. Stops traffic. Have you seen her?"

He had not only seen her, he stalked her. Like a raving lunatic, he followed her footprints when she left work — she was a receptionist in a medical office — and when she walked home. Isabel could not take a step without him following her like a bloodhound.

She, by the way, knew about it and allowed it. But she allowed it with an utterly condescending smile that killed him.

She sees me as a friend! Nothing more than a harmless friend! He ruminated while staring at the ceiling through the early morning hours.

Then he would summon his conclusions, which robbed him of his last hopes of sleep: "What was Machado's secret? What?"

The friend

With a frankness only allowed to be used by a close friend, a childhood friend, Sueli said to Isabel, "Are you going to stay a widow forever? Stop being a fool! Pay attention to Ederval."

"He's just a friend."

"He's obsessed with you. You don't see it because you don't want to."

"I'll say it again. He's just a friend."

"He's even willing to kill himself because of you. Keep your eyes open. Don't carry this cross."

"Eeek! Stop it. Are you blackmailing me?"

Isabel never guessed, but she had hit the nail on the head. Sueli had a hidden agenda. She was in love with Ederval herself. Her heart was stabbed by a crochet hook each time she saw him, and she ran into him every day.

She could not stand seeing him fall into disgrace for the love of another woman. "Why not me? Why not me?" she deliriously repeated.

Such frustration gave Sueli the morbid desire to get revenge, to tell him every small detail, to make him suffer, to compensate for her own suffering. For example, she told him that Isabel was horribly vain. She was always grimacing in the mirror, plastering her face with creams and rejuvenating salves, complaining that she didn't have enough money for plastic surgery.

At that point, Ederval was grinding his teeth, "I have taken a course in facial cosmetology! Diploma and all. I am the scalpless Pitangui[9] of Campo Grande!"

Then he yelled in pure frustration, "Why doesn't she come to me? Why?"

Adding to his suffering, Sueli whispered, "She has a room."

"A room?!"

"A little room, locked tight as a drum. She doesn't let anyone in. I wonder what's inside." Sueli never tired of asking.

Isabel would always change the subject:

"It's none of your business."

"What?" Ederval insisted, his voice strained with desperation to know.

Until one day, Isabel said, "I will only tell you one thing... so you will stop bugging me."

And Sueli said, "So, tell."

"A relic."

"What do you mean?"

"Of my Machado."

Ederval vented his misery with a pungent moan, "Is this how she treats the deceased?"

He found her *post mortem* intimacy of the lowest immorality.

"What relic?" insisted Sueli.

"That I cannot tell. Not even dead."

"She never said?" Ederval asked.

Sueli made a dismissive gesture, he looked away, with the ut-

---

9 An internationally acclaimed Brazilian plastic surgeon.

most certainty that in that dark room, in that mysterious relic, the sacred secret of Machado was held.

The relic

The magazine said that Ana Maria Braga and Xuxa[10] had done it.

"I don't know... Ana Maria Braga," said Sueli with a shudder.
"So what?"
"You don't know?"
"Tell me."
"Well, she looks all plastic. It doesn't count."
"And Xuxa?"
"As far as I know, only her breasts. Now, her face..."
She looked at Isabel. Perfect face, beautiful, not even the shadow of a wrinkle. Who would know she was pushing forty? *Ah, if mine could be like that*, she sighed, and wished to die.
"So? What do you think?"
The magazine told of a revolutionary treatment using chopped ice. One should dip her face in it, hold it down for three minutes, and it was done! Brand new skin, like a baby's butt, at the very least.
"What?" insisted Isabel.
"Do you have ice?"
"In the freezer. I bought it this morning."
"Go get it."
"So you think..."
"Damn it! Just get it. What are you waiting for?"
Everything prepared, Isabel asked before dipping her face in the ice: "Will you keep track of the time?"
"What am I here for?"
Ah, if only she could keep her face immersed until she dropped dead, stiff and cold, and Sueli, finally free of that burden, that anguish, could make a pass at Ederval.

---

10 Two Brazilian celebrities.

Suddenly, well before the three minutes was up, "Ouch!" groaned Isabel. She abruptly pushed away the basin of ice and raised her head.

"Ay!" yelled Sueli, frightened by the sight.

Isabel's mouth was twisted; her features, disfigured, the horror. Worse, she stopped breathing and collapsed on the floor as melodramatically as a silent screen actress.

Panicking — not completely sorry, but still somewhat sad to see her wishes granted so quickly — Sueli ran to ask for help from a neighbor on the floor above, who happened to be a retired nurse.

After examining Isabel, she said, "She's not going to die. You can relax."

"But what was that...?"

"Does she have health insurance?"

"Who gives a rat's ass!"

"Let's put her in a cab and take her to Rocha Faria."

"Oh, my God!"

"You can chill out. Didn't I say she won't die?"

"So, then..."

"She needs to be put under observation. Because of her breathing."

"And the face?"

"It will return to normal after a while."

"But..."

"Work with me here. I'll go with you, but you pay for the cab. You do have cash, don't you?"

As soon as Isabel recovered, Sueli regained her mischievousness, and from the hospital called Ederval.

"I'm rushing over there!" he exclaimed in a thin voice, tightened by fear.

"Go to her apartment first."

"Why, for what?"

"The door is ajar."

"Listen, isn't it better..."

She almost yelled, "Go to the apartment. Don't you see?"

"What?"

"The room. The relic. This is our chance."

The light switch was behind the door. It took him a long time to find it. He waited for his eyes to adjust. The little room had no furniture, not even a miserable little stool. Where could it be?

That's when he spotted it: On one of the side walls, hanging high up almost to the ceiling. It was framed by a white backing and wide border to highlight the colors. It was white with gaudy red stripes.

The relic, at last.

That which maintained the flame lighting Isabel's heart, that which still burned her delicious flesh and left her drowning in memories that she could not confess... nothing more than Machado's *samba-canção* boxer shorts.

Humiliated like a mouse in the sacristy, Ederval painfully squelched his sobs and hurried out, faced with the revolting awareness that he was worth less than a mere pair of underpants, placed in a more-than-questionable frame.

THE RABBI AND THE PSYCHOANALYST[11]

ROSANE CHONCHOL
BRAZIL

11 An excerpt from *The Rabbi and the Psychoanalyst*, KBR, 2012.

Rosane Chonchol is a *carioca*, born and living in Rio de Janei-ro, a third-generation descendent of Jews who emigrated to Brazil from Kiev and Esmirna. She is an artist, a writer, and a psychoanalyst. When she was young, she lived in Europe and was inspired by Lacan, Chaplin, Bergman, Fellini and Woody Allen, resulting in a narrative style that is absolutely original. She mixes a disconcerting concoction of dream and reality, turning the storytelling into a hilarious psycho-analytic session.

*Translated by **A.H. Lin***
*Drawing by **Rosane Chonchol***

the *The Rabbi's black coat* and the *the psychoanalyst couch*

I ndignation. That was what the Grand Rabbi Elias felt when a ridiculous nightmare awoke him in the middle of the night. He dreamt that God had sent him to earth as the Messiah, and he had no more than sixteen hours and fifty minutes to save humanity from extermination. This took place early in the morning on a Saturday, the Jewish Sabbath, the day that the Father chose to rest.

What can I do in sixteen hours? he thought, deeply distressed. He decided to call his friend, Dr. Solomon, psychoanalyst emeritus, recognized for both his seriousness and his orthodoxy. They had been friends in their student days, when Elias had been preparing to become a rabbi.

Elias told Solomon his dream:

"Sitting in a big armchair, Jehovah said to me, 'Don't kneel before me, not before anyone. Don't just lie there. Go back to your studies and try to accomplish something. Don't count on me. I decided thousands of years ago, the world ends on this Sabbath. But humanity cultivates a dream of salvation. Everyone hopes for it, but not me. Then again, I'm immortal.'"

Elias told the psychoanalyst of his indignation:

"What an absurdity that Jehovah would say this to me! Help me, Solomon. Am I insane? Give me an answer fast. I have only sixteen hours and fifty minutes to act. And fifteen minutes have already passed."

Solomon responded, "Elias, take a pill and go to bed. We'll talk tomorrow. I have nothing more to tell you now."

Elias forsook the customary, calm, composed demeanor befitting a Grand Rabbi and said, "You will be the first to die. Do you understand?"

"'Yes, I understand that you want me to be the first to die."

It began to thunder incessantly. Solomon grew frightened and thought, *What can I do? What will the writings of Freud tell me?* He hung up the phone and went to the library. He paged through some articles on psychoanalysis without being able to concentrate on what he was reading. Feeling a stabbing pain in his stomach, he got dressed and went to Elias's house. It was seven in the morning, and the sun already shone over the city.

He rang the doorbell. The Rabbi's wife opened the door with a look of despair. Seeing him, she said, "Good, you've come! Elias prayed all night and warned the family that today was the end of the world."

My God, the Rabbi has gone crazy once and for all, he thought.

"Come talk to your friend," Elias's wife told him.

However, Elias refused and said that Jehovah had told him, "Don't lie down." He decided that to join Solomon, he would have to lie down, lie down on the analyst's couch.

"I can't be your patient, just as I can't kneel in front of anyone. Can I even walk? If I try to stand up, I will fall. I am paralyzed. My legs hurt. I have to save the world. I am the Messiah and I can't even walk! Solomon, protect me. I am helpless. God sent me a message, only this: humanity said that I have to save it."

"You're wrong, Elias. Humanity chose me. Only I can save it. I became a psychoanalyst for this reason. I am the Messiah."

The Grand Rabbi rose from the couch without help and, relieved, said, "I am better. I no longer have any pain. I can walk and do what I wish. The problem is yours. Leave me now. Today is my day of rest, but it will also be my day of celebration. Go away."

Solomon didn't move. He stood still. Nervously, he took a cigar and asked for a cup of coffee.

"No, no, Solomon. Get out. Go away," and he pushed him out the door.

The psychoanalyst did not accept being thrown out. "Damn you and your religion! You are crazy!"

The Rabbi smiled. "The problem is yours, my friend. I am doing fine."

Dr. Solomon left quite upset. His watch said nine o'clock. He should already be at the office. Though Jewish, he worked on Saturday. He swallowed a sedative and entered the office late. His first patient, a beautiful woman of thirty, had already waited a half hour and was hysterical, of course.

Infuriated, she said, "I agree to come early on a Saturday for my session. I get here, and you aren't here! I am angry. I've lost my time here. The world is going to end and my psychoanalyst doesn't even show up to see me!"

"Come in, Margot. Relax. Lie down on the couch and talk. Today you tell me that the world is going to end. Yesterday you ended the session talking about the hate that you feel because your father married your mother and you wish to kill him."

"It happened, Dr. Solomon. My father had a stroke last night, and now not only can I not marry him, but I have to keep a secret he told me before he died. I certainly can never tell anyone what he told me, "My daughter, I am the Messiah." Now I am in a hurry and must go. Reporters from the *State Journal* await the statement I will give concerning the death of my father, the Messiah. You have nothing to interpret. Don't talk to me about castration anxiety, Oedipus or phallic superiority, or even omnipotence. I don't believe in any of that any more. He died saying he was the Messiah. He, a very religious man and a Christian, would not sin like this. My father never lied. He died as the Messiah. The world is going to end in a few hours. I am going to pay and leave."

"You are wrong," said the psychoanalyst. "The world is not going to end. It ended for him and being identified with him, you think you died with him."

"No, doctor. I didn't die. You died. I am going to tell you how I know what is to come. It is your fault. You did not save my father. I asked, implored for years, over hundreds of sessions, 'Don't kill my father.' But you killed him. You will bear the consequences."

The analyst was desperate. He did not understand. "I didn't kill your father. You killed him in your fantasy, but unfortunately he really died. My daughter, cry, vent, but don't abandon treatment."

"Why not? The world is going to end even if I would like to continue coming! There is no tomorrow. It ends. I want to end my treatment and pay up." She took out the money and handed it to Dr. Solomon, saying, "Don't fool yourself. There is no tomorrow." And she left.

The psychoanalyst was stricken. He turned on the radio to distract himself. Today he had already lost his old friend, the Rabbi, whom he greatly respected. And Margot, his dear patient, despite her serious Oedipal complex, poor thing. He listened to the news:

"The Pope alerted humanity that the world will end today."

Deep in thought, he did not understand what was happening, so many coincidences! The doorbell rang. It was Joe, his twelve o'clock patient, a sixteen-year-old.

The boy entered and said, "Dr. Solomon, there is nothing else we can do. My tablet predicted that today is the last day. The atomic bomb will fall today. It will be the apocalypse. Together with the bomb, we will all be tripping in an orgy of cocaine. It will rain coke all over the world."

"What coke, son, Coca-Cola?"

"No, cocaine. They will use the atomic bomb to destroy the city of Santa Cruz de la Sierra, the huge reservoir of holy dust. The world will end under a white rain. Can you imagine how great it's going to be? At least I can die while tripping. It is what I always wanted!"

My God! thought Solomon. *This is really my day. Everyone around me is going insane.*

"Knock it off, Joe. Go away. I can't take any more today."

The boy left, and Solomon asked his secretary for a cup of coffee.

She said, "What coffee, Doctor! Do something. I have confidence in you. Today is the last day of life on earth. I love you. Only you can save the world."

"How? It's the end of the world. One more nutcase. Will this be my destiny, to suffer the crazies? Even the Grand Rabbi went bonkers..."

Just then the telephone range. It was Elias:

"How about it, Solomon, have you taken some measures to save the world?"

The analyst hung up on his friend, the respected Rabbi. He took another sedative. Leaving without even eating lunch, he went the hospital where he worked in the afternoon. There, they could tell him as much as they wanted that the world was going to end. The patients were diagnosed psychotic by competent medical boards.

But despite his apparent calm as he drove, Solomon became upset as he thought about his day, lost control of himself, and arrived screaming. He joined the clientele of the sophisticated sanitarium, a very fancy and ridiculously expensive hospital for only the rich. As a matter of fact, since the cure was so expensive, the patients were poor by the time they left.

The analyst yelled, "The world is going to end today! We have three more hours."

The crazies were laughing themselves to death. "Dr. Solomon is delirious!"

"You have to help me. The world ends today, only you don't know it. You are crazy." He began to cry convulsively.

Everyone pitied him. They called the nurse, and she called the psychiatrist on duty, who immediately gave him an injection of Valium and told him to calm down.

Solomon told him, "The world is ending today! The nurses, I, even the desk clerk know about it. Russia broke the seal and already gave notice that they would launch the atomic bomb at the same time as the United States. The two countries synchronized the attack to fire in unison. This way, no one is to blame. No one will go first. It was a bilateral nuclear pact, but the patients don't believe it. These wretches are out of touch. Leave them in peace. The news was on the radio ten minutes ago, counting down exactly one hour until the end of the world."

Solomon ran out, screaming like a frightened animal that had suffered an incurable injury, "Fifty minutes left. Fifty minutes left. The fifty minutes are chasing me. Just as the Rabbi said, ''Sixteen hours and fifty minutes." And I wasted the day. Now, all that is left is the time of one analytic session. What am I going to do in fifty minutes!? What can I in this amount of time?"

In a low voice, Dr. Henrique called, "Dr. Solomon. Dr. Solomon. One analytic hour!"

"No! No! What analytic hour?! I don't want to die. I can't analyze anyone in my last fifty minutes."

Dr. Henrique, former university professor with doctorates in philosophy, economics, and political science, and a patient at the hospital for the past five years, said, "Doctor, you know my history better than anyone. I already foresaw everything. For this they expelled me from the university where I was lecturing, and my family locked me up. We still have fifty minutes. Lie down on the couch in my room and we will have an analytic session. We will talk about your mother, your Oedipal complex, your castration anxiety, and all the rest. You will be my patient. It will be the ultimate analytic session."

Helpless, Solomon lay down on the couch and said, "Henrique, everyone knew except me."

He heard nothing more except laughter, the inmates' laughter echoing through the hospital and also Jehovah's, exploding in bursts.

THE GREAT LIE[12]

MAURICIO WROTS
BRAZIL

12 An excerpt from *Moishele and the Flowerless Rosebush*, KBR, 2014.

Mauricio Wrots lives in Rio de Janeiro. He started his career as a journalist in the discontinued satirical newspaper called *O Pasquim*, becoming well-known for its criticism directed at the military dictatorship. At Globo television, he worked as a writer for a satirical show called *Satiricom*. At the Educational channel in Rio de Janeiro, he created and coordinated the program *Tribunal da História* (*The Court of History*). He published a collection of short stories, *A Relatividade da Infidelidade* (*The Relativism of Infidelity*). With *Moishele and the Flowerless Rosebush*, his first novel published by KBR, he has had the opportunity to meet his Jewish roots.

Translated by **Adriana Jorge**

The great idea, or rather, the great "lie," came to him on a Sunday, at an amusement park called Quinta da Boa Vista, a traditional family activity at the time, while he was passing by a photography stall, where the photographer, through a photo montage, placed the clients' pictures in an airplane cabin, flying over the clouds.

Mendel talked to Machado, the portraitist, and, paying well, hired his services for an unusual task, a very ingenious plan that would touch Yacov's weakness. He paid for half of the service in advance and set all the details. The next day, wearing his best suit, Mendel placed himself next to the biggest and most luxurious jewelry shop on Ouvidor Street. Feigning seriousness, he posed as the owner, and, on the other side of the street, Machado photographed the scene, quickly, before someone from the store could show up. Then, it was necessary to develop the photographic plate with an adjustment required by Mendel: Machado should scrape off the original name of the jewelry shop and place a false name: "ROSENSTRAUCH BROTHERS, JEWELLERS."

The montage was so perfect that, for a few seconds, Mendel felt like the real owner of the establishment. The brightness of a sunny day even allowed the mixed showcase within the shop window to be seen.

Mendel talked to no one about his plan, not even his wife. After all, they would probably doubt his sanity. He would send a letter to Germany, telling Yacov about the acquisition of the jewelry shop, saying he hadn't mentioned anything because it was somewhat uncertain. They would become partners, as already written on the shop window. He hoped his brother would bite the bait and be courageous enough to sell his small business, even at a loss.

It was all a fantasy, of course, but Mendel considered it a necessary lie. Moved by the supernatural message, he was sure that Yacov was at risk and that the Nuremberg Nazi Laws, revoking the citizenship of the Jews, were just a foretaste of what was to come, even though the 1936 Olympics Games in Germany, temporarily softened the persecution, conveying the false impression that the worst had already happened. His brother's reaction after arriving in Brazil, and becoming aware of the farce, was a problem to be solved later. At that moment, what really mattered was saving these lives from a threat that he, in Brazil, felt closer than those living in the heart of the Third Reich.

Mendel also included in the letter some pictures of downtown Rio de Janeiro, with its Europeanized streets and avenues, showing his brother that he wouldn't arrive in the middle of a jungle, with snakes and naked Indians.

The letter arrived in Berlin in early July 1938. Looking at the picture of "his" jewelry shop in Brazil, with a great shop window full of showcases, and noticing his brother's and the bystanders' elegance, Yacov got really excited. He shared his excitement with his wife and they discussed the pros and cons. According to the Nazi laws, leaving Berlin basically meant losing your accumulated capital, that is to say, the property and the goods which assured your survival. The Reich imposed legitimate limitations, absurd onerous conditions for the Jews who decided to leave, forcing them to sell their assets at a great loss.

Another drawback included getting exit visas in Germany and entry visas in Brazil, besides the evil German bureaucracy concerning anything related to the Semites. However, Mendel had added a PS in the letter, saying that Yacov just needed to agree, and he, Mendel, would be responsible for enabling the trip.

Up to that moment, Yacov had endured with resignation all the prohibitions imposed by the regime, some highly ridiculous, such as visiting the zoo, a privilege allowed only to Aryans. Yacov disdained: "I can do just great without those animals!" Nevertheless, he felt sorry for leaving his beautiful city. He couldn't understand the reason for such a rush; after all, Hitler wasn't "that Pharaoh who ordered the slaughter of innocent people."

Mendel insisted on an immediate answer. Yacov tried to resist, but he was concerned about his brother finding another partner. Hesitant, he didn't know he was dancing over an abyss: "Haven't the Nazis done enough against us? What else can they do? *Pogroms*... massacres... belong to the past, in Russia, in Ukraine, in Poland, not in a modern Western world. We are in Berlin, in 1938." His survival instinct was not that good.

He kept postponing an answer. He carefully listened to his wife's relatives, born in Germany, other businessmen and friends. *Moreover, at the slightest sign of risk, I could return to Poland, my home country, very close and safe*, he thought. Yacov's wife's family didn't welcome the idea of leaving. Would she, Erika, a native of Berlin, be able to live in the "Brazilian jungle"? And what about Yacov, an assimilated Pole? Could he survive living as a fish out of water in such an exotic and faraway place? It was a dilemma.

He could go on living without the citizenship, without the zoo, without the public offices and, of course, without having sex with an Aryan woman, a criminal act that could even end up with the death penalty. "All these have always been a luxury for our people."

But the picture of that magnificent jewelry shop on a major commercial street in Rio de Janeiro was stuck in his mind.

Some people Yacov talked to, on the other hand, envied his luck, because the maximum they would get right now, through really hard work, was an exit visa to China, the only country that had kept its doors opened to the Jews.

A far more serious situation, commercially speaking, was the losing of Aryan clients, as they were prohibited by law from entering the stores with a "J" on the shop front, making business impossible and forcing the Jews to sell low-priced jewelry. Fixing pieces was the only activity that ensured making some money — his thoughts were coming and going, as usual. On one hand, he could live well as his brother's partner in Rio de Janeiro; on the other hand, giving up the comfort of one of the best cities in Europe was painful.

In Brazil, Mendel was truly worried about the lack of news from his brother. He still believed in Vicentina's vision. Yacov should have quickly become aware he was at risk, but it didn't happen and time was flying. He decided to add another bait, an extra warranty: If nothing happened, if the Nazis let the Jews alone, even with so many restrictions, Yacov could go back to Germany free of any cost, and with a nice nest egg as well. And it was like that, using such attractive terms, that he finally convinced the couple.

The young couple faced the proposal as a leisure trip, without expenses and financial risk. They also requested all the privileges a luxury cruise could offer — they wouldn't travel on a ship full of scared immigrants — promptly accepted by Mendel, who noticed the time was going down the drain every time they exchanged letters.

They finally decided to come. Relieved, Mendel had another battle ahead: To get entry visas for the couple.

President Getulio Vargas, at the time, was "flirting" with the Nazis, and had even authorized the extradition of a Jewish woman, Olga, *Luis Carlos Prestes's*[13] wife, who ended up being executed; and his "eugenic" immigration policy was object of secret circular letters sent to all consulates, prohibiting the entry of the "unwelcome" — a diplomatic euphemism concerning the Semite immigrants.

Mendel thought, even without concrete evidence, that something really bad would happen in Germany soon. He was aware of the Brazilian meanders and shortcuts, the so-called *jeitinho brasileiro*,[14] you just needed to know someone influential in the government and mobilize him or her in the necessary urgency. But he didn't know any politician, not even a council member. He needed to quickly find a way to bribe someone; many visas were bought behind the curtain. If he couldn't directly approach the big shot, he would have to do it through low-ranking, that meant, looking for someone who knew someone and so on.

He thought about Matilde, an exuberant brunette, who used to buy expensive jewelry in his shop without a known source of income. Mendel, discreetly, knew the origin of such resources: They came from a member of the president's security guard, someone who was part of the group headed by the black man called Gregório Fortunato, Getúlio's "Black Angel," one of the most powerful characters of the Republic. Mendel decided to go to her house.

---

13 The controversial leader of the Brazilian Communist Party (PCB).
14 Portuguese, meaning "Brazilian way."

There, he unfolded the black velvet on the sofa. He selected the most beautiful bracelets, earrings, necklaces and golden rings. His client's eyes were shining, pretty much the same way the eyes of a *bandeirante*[15] shone when he found tourmalines and mistook them for emeralds. Amazed, she pressed her hands against her chest and choked on the words. She hesitated to try a ring or close a bracelet.

"This is all so beautiful, Mendel, but it's not for me! I've been your client for quite a while, you know how far I can go," Matilde reacted.

"Choose a bracelet, a ring and a pair of earrings," Mendel replied.

"Choose for what? I won't be able to buy them anyway."

"You don't have to pay. In return, I want you to do me a favor."

Matilde smiled in a playful way, somewhat malicious.

"What favor, Mendel?"

Mendel understood the joke.

"No, Matilde, that's not the case... The favor I need is from your friend Teixeira, the one from Gregório's group."

Matilde got excited:

"Teixeira will do anything I tell him to."

Mendel gave her the jewelry. In a few days, the Brazilian visas were issued, and in Berlin, there were no difficulties, thanks to the good diplomatic relations between Brazil and Germany. When Yacov decided to travel, the racial laws and the anti-Semitic persecution hadn't reached their peak, there hadn't been bloodshed, except in isolated cases.

On board, the couple lived dream days. It was the sophisticated honeymoon they never had, in the first class of a comfortable transatlantic ship, and Yacov was promised a great and prestigious commercial position, as the partner of one of the main jewelry shops in Rio, according to his brother's letters.

He was somehow puzzled with Mendel's sudden progress. Being a non-established trader, he had suddenly reached such status in a short time, surprising his brother with the partnership propo-

---

15 A Brazilian explorer in the colonial era.

sal. *Things that happen in Brazil...* he thought, like the stories he had heard about.

Just a few days before, in Berlin, his wife had been standing in lines to get some rationed food. The ship, however, was an oasis. A cabin, fine wines, varied gastronomy, and Strauss waltzes: pure Aryan treatment. On the high seas, during the journey, blended with the other passengers, Yacov even forgot about what it meant to be a Jew. At a particular time, as a spontaneous reaction, he even responded to a greeting of an official, who, in a friendly way, stretched out his arm, using the Hitler greeting.

In the middle of the Atlantic, he didn't get news about international crises; actually, he didn't get any kind of news, and such isolation made him create an illusion that the world was a still lake. But while Yacov and Erika were waltzing in the majestic ballroom of the ship, under the splendor of gigantic crystal chandeliers, to the rhythm of the waltz "Tales from the Vienna Woods," at the daybreak of the November 10, 1938, in Berlin, the Viennese Joseph Goebbels was mobilizing the SA, the paramilitary group of the Nazi Party. He was planning retaliatory actions for a murder in Paris, in which a young Jew had killed an employee of the German Embassy.

While whirling and drinking champagne, the couple had no idea that, at that very moment, in Berlin, during the so-called "Night of Broken Glass" (*Kristallnacht*) — due to the shards of shattered glass on the ground reflecting the moonlight — broken glasses from the window of their jewelry shop was lying in the middle of the street. Window panes of hundreds of other shops owned by the Jews would be shattered by the hysterical crowd, who extended the barbarism to burning synagogues, killing, hurting, and taking millions of members of their community to a prison in Dachau.

Unaware of the attack, the couple arrived a few days later at the wharf in Rio de Janeiro, where Mendel was waiting for them. Deeply moved, the brothers hugged each other. But Yacov didn't have a clue why his brother was hugging him so tight. And why was he crying? They complained a lot about the hot weather. While they were in Mendel's Ford 34 driving to Grajaú, the burning hood made them sweat in their European outfits. They glanced at each other, showing some regret; perhaps they wouldn't get used to that heat. If they could not, they would return to the wharf and take the same ship back to Germany, but, soon, they would know it was no longer possible to set foot on German soil without being at risk of death.

They asked themselves: *Was it worth it coming to such inhospitable place, even considering the great financial advantage?* After being lodged and rested from the trip, it was time to face the shock of reality. While they were having an afternoon snack, Yacov's feared question came up:

"When are we going to the jewelry shop?"

Erika, uneasy, already wanted to know, if they wished, how they would go back, giving her husband squinting, accusatory looks. Mendel, looking serious, observed the couple's naive ignorance: They weren't aware of the massacre in Berlin yet. He had not said anything.

He simply picked up the newspapers of the Jewish press and gave them to Yacov. The atrocities of November 10th, which caused the death of 91 Jews, sent millions to the Dachau concentration camp and burned and destroyed hundreds of synagogues, were the headlines on the first pages; the stores had been looted and the shop windows crashed, while the couple had enjoyed the security and comfort of a transatlantic ship.

After reading the news about the gloomy dawn, Yacov cried. He thought about his loved ones there, such as Erika's parents, and he was sure that a new and even more terrible Hitlerism wave had started. He imagined the golden letters on his small shop window turned into uncountable pieces of broken glass. He was also aware that he had narrowly escaped the brutality against the Jews, which marked the beginning of the history of the Holocaust.

If Mendel hadn't insisted and proposed a partnership, he would have stayed in Berlin. He got goose bumps just by imagining where and how he would be. Germany was over for him. Slowly, he was adapting to the blow, and trying to get used to the surroundings. But, again, he asked about the jewelry shop.

It was the moment of truth. Mendel had even rehearsed an apologetic tone, but he took courage and went straight to the point, without hesitating:

"Yacov, I want you to forgive me, but this jewelry shop doesn't exist. It was an argument I used to bring you and your wife to Brazil, to save you both from annihilation."

Yacov was reluctant to understand his explanation. He couldn't believe it. He thought Mendel was joking.

"Mendel, how could you come up with such a story? What about the picture you sent me?"

"It was a photo montage, I asked a professional to change the name on the shop window."

"You're mad, brother! Why such a lie?"

Mendel showed him, again, the headlines.

"To save your life, to keep you out of a concentration camp!"

Yacov was still confused.

"But no one knew about it! Not even me, who used to live in the Reich. How did you know about the *pogrom* in such advance? Is Mendel Rosenstrauch a prophet?"

Mendel wasn't sure about his answer. It would sound ridiculous for a newcomer from Germany, Einstein's homeland, to accept that everything had happened because of Vicentina, who, while serving breakfast, had glimpsed a picture of the couple and had a vision in which both were being beaten. But he didn't evade his brother question, he wouldn't care if he laughed at him. Yacov was safe, and it was all that mattered.

"I'm not a prophet, but Vicentina is."

"And who is Vicentina? A woman with a crystal ball?"

"Nope! Vicentina is our maid, that woman you saw working in the kitchen. She belongs to a spiritualist lineage of African slaves, and some practitioners of this religion are clairvoyants. When she saw your picture, she fell into a trance, and had a vision of you two lying on the floor, your bodies bleeding, covered in broken glass; and she pointed at the armband with the swastika on the stamp of the letter, saying your aggressors were wearing it as well. Reading the newspapers, we know that this really happened to thousands of Jews, all staged by the Nazis under the pretext of revenging the murder of a German diplomat in Paris. Now, I ask you: How could she know that? What about the swastika? She had no idea these things even existed. She simply saw the man and the woman in the picture being slaughtered, and I didn't despise a warning coming from someone so humble, I couldn't be that arrogant; even facing my friends' mockery, I didn't give up taking you two out of there. And again I ask you: If it weren't for Vicentina, where would both of you be right now? Besides that, the Kabbalah teaches us not to despise certain signs, certain warnings, no matter where they come from."

Yacov was relieved that he hadn't been taken by the vortex of the *Kristallnacht,* but he was frustrated because the jewelry shop in Brazil, which fed his dreams for a short time, didn't exist. He couldn't help admiring his brother's trick to bring him to the country, since he wouldn't have emigrated without that photo montage; and, if his ambition hadn't defeated his convenience, he would have kept living there, hoping the persecution would stop for a while, as had happened in 1936 during the Olympic Games in Berlin.

Without the possibility of returning, he had to adapt to the new place. The unbearable heat made him sweat all the time, forcing him to use equally unbearable fans, which made his wife complain because they messed her hair. He missed the times snow blocked his door and the paths. *It was so good to live in Berlin...*

Actually, Yacov thought the clairvoyant's story was also made up by Mendel. But he remained silent about that. Neither had he pictured himself selling rings, earrings, necklaces and golden chains in government agencies, the type of job that was waiting for him. He thought this work was somewhat humiliating, as he had been a small, but established, trader in one of the biggest European capitals.

Two opposite poles determined his feelings towards Mendel: Consciously, he was grateful because he was saved from the hordes of Hitlerism; on the other hand, now out of risk, he still suffered due to the false commercial expectation, a good lie that had broken his resistance and made him cross the ocean. He asked himself: *Couldn't it have been done in a different way?* And he, himself, answered: *No! Without the picture of the shop I would have never come...*

Mendel didn't pressure him. Yacov was trying to adapt to the place and the weather, a hard task for someone who used to living in cultured Berlin. It was completely different if compared to the immigrants from Poland, who, in most cases — including Mendel's —, came from remote regions where electricity was not common, the opportunities were very scarce, and the anti-Semitism tradition originated from centuries of Christianity. In Germany, from way back, the Enlightenment had taken the Jews out of the ghetto.

But Berlin should be forgotten. Germany was, now, Hitler's hatred. Erika wrote a letter to her relatives living in Buenos Aires — Argentina was prospering thanks to wheat exports and, mainly, to the meat. So, an invitation was made: Why don't you come to the Argentinean capital, known as the "Paris of South America"? When Yacov heard about a snowy region in Argentina, and saw pictures of ski tracks in Bariloche, he was very excited, and approved the idea.

They had spent only three months in Brazil, before deciding to go. Erika was constantly feeling nauseous and a doctor's appointment cleared the doubt: She was pregnant. On the eve of their departure, the incredulous Yacov, appreciating the beauty of the rosebushes, meditated, still intrigued, on that mysterious and absurd story, thinking about the circumstances that had led mother and son to Mendel's house.

While "talking" to the rosebushes, with a grin, he repeated his own name: "Rosenstrauch." How could he possibly understand the enigma of that woman whom Mendel believed, of Mendel's refusal to give up until they were out of risk, a risk which, for being stubborn, neither Erika nor he wanted to face, even after listening to the *Führer*'s threatening speeches, or seeing the brown shirts — the Nazi storm troopers — passing by his door?

He shivered, while realizing that Vicentina, through intuition, hunch or revelation — it didn't really matter — saved not only the couple, but also the baby who was on the way. He finally gave up finding an explanation.

On the day of departure, Mendel drove them to the wharf. But before leaving the house, while saying goodbye, under surprised looks, the quiet and unsociable Erika hugged Vicentina with tears in her eyes and kissed the boy in her arms. She took off her golden chain with a Star of David and put it on him.

Yacov and Erika travelled without knowing that Vicentina had had another vision, which she only told Mendel:

"Those men burned the lady's piano."

Mendel asked his sister-in-law if she used to have a piano, but he chose not to tell anything.

"Yes, I did! It's at my parent's house on Prinzregentenstrasse, I wish I had it here with me!"

It was one of the most aristocratic streets in Berlin.

What about the house? Did the vandals burn it too? Mendel was concerned about Erika's parents, but Vicentina didn't say anything about them. Months later, through a letter from his brother, he learned that the piano, the house and her parents had not escaped. The beautiful house was burned to the ground, and her parents had been taken to Dachau.

In parallel, causing great concern, the fast increase of the actions against the Jews in Germany, anticipating even darker actions, made Mendel feel proud for not being arrogant and for believing the "Kabbalistic" message coming from a humble creature of esoteric creed. And it all happened because that day, in front of his house, he had protected Moishele and Vicentina with his umbrella.

It was not a simple coincidence. If he had arrived later, he wouldn't have met them, he wouldn't have listened to the message about the flowerless rosebush, he wouldn't have hired Vicentina, she wouldn't have had the vision about the Night of Broken Glass, and he wouldn't have saved his brother. From then on, Faiga gave in, and accepted that Moishele and Mendel would make their own history.